D1314328

Finding-Out Books

Plants on the Go

A Book About Seed Dispersal

By ELEANOR B. HEADY

Illustrated by SUSAN SWAN

Parents' Magazine Press/New York

Library of Congress Cataloging in Publication Data

Heady, Eleanor B.
  Plants on the go.

  (Finding-out books)
  SUMMARY: Describes the characteristics of various
plants, their process of reproduction, and the many
ways seeds travel over the earth.
    1. Plants—Reproduction—Juvenile literature.
2. Seeds—Dissemination—Juvenile literature.
[1. Plants—Reproduction.   2. Seeds—Dispersal]
I. Swan, Susan Burrows, illus.   II. Title.
QK825.H37   582′.05′6   74-665
ISBN 0-8193-0726-2

Contents

1 Plants

Plants grow all around us. Many things that we use every day are plants or parts of plants. The rosebush in a garden, the carrots in a grocery store, the wood that some people burn in their fireplaces, the cotton in our clothes, all grew as plants.

We find plants growing wherever there is soil, even in sidewalk cracks.

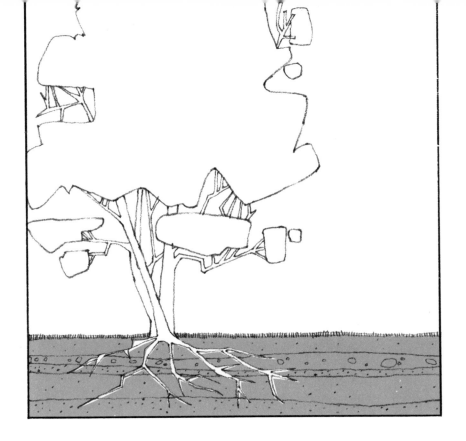

Plants cover vacant lots and roadsides, fields and forests, city parks and gardens. They grow in our houses in pots of soil. Plants have flowers that we like because of their bright colors and sweet smells.

Plants grow in the soil. Their roots reach down into the earth. A plant's roots do two very important things. First, they anchor, or hold, the plant in place, helping even the tallest tree to stand upright. Second, roots feed a plant. They take water and minerals from the soil. Plants use minerals for food. Water runs into the soil. It dissolves the minerals and mixes with them. Tiny roots soak up this mixture. From the smallest roots, the water and minerals move into the larger roots, up the plant stems, and into the leaves.

Leaves are living factories. In them are tiny bits of a green material called *chlorophyll.* Chlorophyll uses the water-dissolved minerals from the soil; *carbon-dioxide,* a gas, from the air; and energy, or heat and light, from the sun and makes sugars and starches, called *carbohydrates.*

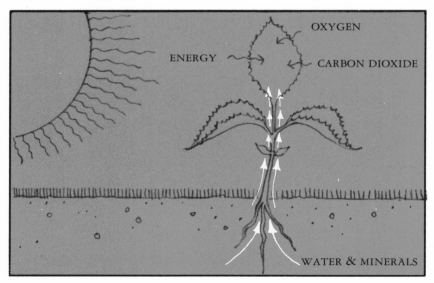

PHOTOSYNTHESIS

This making of sugars and starches is called *photosynthesis.* It helps plants grow large because they can manufacture more plant material to add to their own bodies.

Animals and people eat plants. Think of the many things you eat every day that are plants or plant parts. Lettuce, potatoes, apples, bread made from wheat, all come from plants.

Cows eat hay, grass, and grain, which are plants, and we drink the milk from these cows. Cheese is made from milk. So is ice cream.

The meat we eat is the flesh of animals, who ate plants to make the meat. Only plants can manufacture food for animals and people.

ROSEBUD

Plants are more than roots, stems, and leaves. Every plant must have some way to *reproduce,* or start new plants. This important job is done by flowers. Flowers make the seeds from which most plants grow.

Let us look at a flower. It has a number of different parts. The first thing we see are the showy, brightly colored petals. But petals are only one part of a flower.

Flowering weeds grow in vacant lots and along roadsides. We can see flowers in gardens and windowboxes. Seeds grow in these flowers. The way flowers make seeds is one of nature's wonders. Soon we will discover how it works.

ZINNIA

MARIGOLD

2 Flowers

Flowers grow in many colors, sizes, and shapes. They may look very different from each other, but they all have certain definite parts. Some blossoms, such as zinnias or marigolds, are really many small flowers growing close together. Perhaps you have a geranium in a pot on your windowsill at home or at school. If you look closely at the flower, you will see that the one big bloom is a number of smaller flowers all growing from the top of one stem.

GERANIUM

9

For a closer look at a flower, pick one from the garden. If you do not have a garden, maybe a florist will give you a faded flower. A large single blossom, such as a hollyhock or perhaps a petunia, is best.

Ask a grown-up to cut your flower with a sharp knife, starting at the stem and cutting upward through the center. The stem swells into a bowl or vase shape. Green, leaf-like *sepals* grow from the outside of the base. Inside the circle of sepals are white or colored petals. These grow around tiny, thread-like stamens, each tipped with yellow *pollen.* In the center of the stamens is the *ovary,* the holder for the seeds. A slender tube, called the *style,* grows from the center of the ovary. It flares out into a sticky upper end, the *stigma.*

In some flowers, such as iris, the ovary grows under the petals.

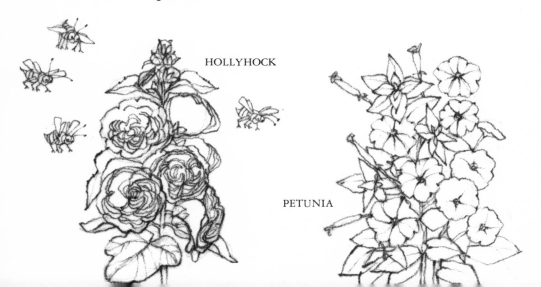

HOLLYHOCK

PETUNIA

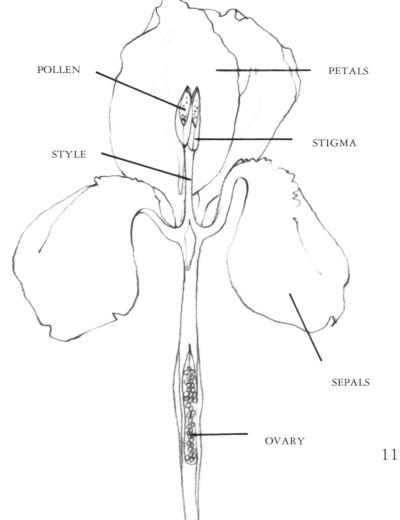

POLLEN

PETALS

STYLE

STIGMA

SEPALS

OVARY

11

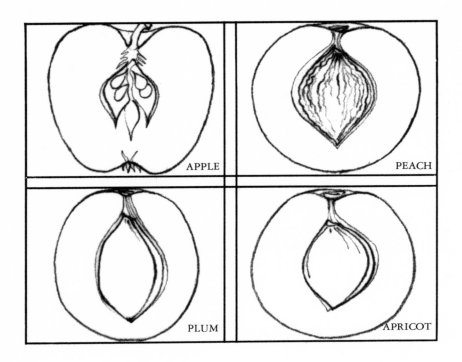

APPLE

PEACH

PLUM

APRICOT

Some flowers make only one seed. Others make many. A peach blossom makes one peach seed. An apple blossom makes one apple with many seeds inside it. Ask someone to cut across an apple. Look at its many seeds. Now do the same with a peach, plum, or apricot. See how one seed grows inside each of these fruits.

Flowers need help to make seeds. And they have ways to get the help they need. But first let us find out how flowers grow into seeds.

If a flower is to make one or many seeds it must

be *fertilized.* A flower is fertilized when a pollen grain sticks to the top of the stigma and sends its tube with *sperm* cells down into the ovary. Most flowers need pollen from another flower to fertilize their ovaries.

After a flower is fertilized, the ovary begins to swell with the new seed forming inside it.

But how do you suppose pollen gets from one flower to another? We shall see the many ways pollen moves from flower to flower.

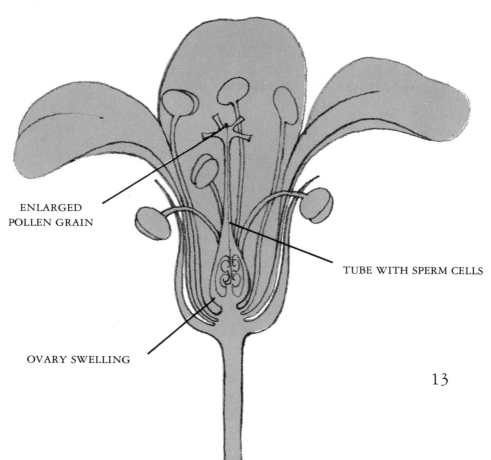

ENLARGED
POLLEN GRAIN

TUBE WITH SPERM CELLS

OVARY SWELLING

3 Flower Helpers

If you stand under the branches of a blooming fruit tree and listen, what do you hear? That buzzing, humming sound is made by bees as they visit flower after flower.

Each bee sits on one flower for a moment, puts his long snout into the center, and sucks. He is getting nectar, or sweetness. When a bee has collected all he can carry he flies home to the hive. There he leaves his load to turn into honey.

 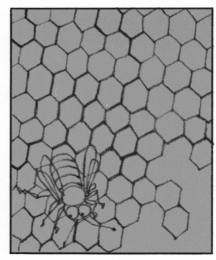

CLOVER   ALFALFA

Bees do more than make honey. They help flowers to grow seeds. To get nectar each bee must burrow among the flower's stamens that are covered with dusty, sticky pollen. Pollen grains stick to his legs and fuzzy sides. He leaves some of the pollen on the next flower he visits. Bees help spread pollen from one flower to another.

Farmers sometimes rent colonies of bees to help *pollinate,* or bring pollen, so that crops will make seeds. Clover and alfalfa seeds are often grown with help from hired bees.

If you take a close look at a pansy, you will notice how the colors on its face lead to its yellow center. This is a target for the bee, leading him to the nectar and pollen-filled center.

PANSY   15

Night-flying moths pollinate some flowers. These flowers are often white or some other light color so that moths can see them in the dark. They send out a perfume that the moths like. Some flower shapes fit the long nectar-sucking tubes of the moths that visit them. One flower pollinated by moths is the common garden phlox.

Have you ever seen a hummingbird suck nectar from one flower and flit away to another? Hummingbirds prefer brightly colored flowers, especially red ones. Like a bee, each little bird sees the nectar-filled center and flies to it. Pushing his long, slender beak down into the blossom, he sucks up the sweet nectar with his tiny, tube-shaped tongue. Grains of pollen stick in the nectar clinging to his beak. He drops or brushes some of this pollen onto the next flower he visits.

In Europe and in North and South America, bats pollinate some night-blooming flowers. Bats find these blooms because they smell sweet, sour, or rotten. Bats pollinate the flowers of the giant cactus of Arizona.

Besides bees, moths, birds, and bats, flowers have another very important helper. Many grasses and some trees shed pollen so light that the wind blows it about. It sails across the country high in the sky, even far out to sea. Finally some of it comes to rest on other flowers, many miles from the places where it grew.

Many wind-pollinated plants have small green or greenish-yellow flowers. They have no need for bright colors and large showy petals to attract bees, birds, and moths. They need no strong odors.

Try to find some tall grass by the roadside, in a corner of a park or garden, or in a vacant lot. Be sure to choose a grass plant that is still green, one with a spike growing from its center. If you look carefully you may see the green, yellow, or perhaps dark-colored flowers. These tiny flowers look almost like the rest of the grass plant. They have no bright petals, only stamens covered with fine pollen dust.

Pick the grass flower stem. Shake the pollen onto a piece of white paper. Now pick up the paper, but be careful not to spill the pollen. Blow across the paper. What happens? Think what a brisk wind, so much stronger than your breath, would do to scatter the grass pollen.

Wind mixes and stirs pollen grains. Plants that pollinate a certain grass or a tree may grow many miles away from it.

Evergreen trees, called *conifers,* or cone bearers, depend on the wind to pollinate their flowers. They usually grow close together in a forest. Their green and yellow-green flowers bear great masses of pollen. When the wind blows through the trees, the fine pollen grains ride the breeze to fall on the sticky stigmas of other blossoms.

As spring moves on to summer, the fertilized blossoms grow. They look like small green fruits. Finally, as autumn nears, they turn into brown cones. Their sections open to let the dry seeds drift away. Then the empty cones fall to the ground.

4 Seeds

After a bee, bird, moth, bat, or the wind drops a
pollen grain on a flower, a tube with a special sperm
cell grows down the style to fertilize the ovary. A
seed begins. The seed gets slowly larger, fed by the
parent plant. (See picture, page 13.) Finally, the seed
is fully grown, or mature. It becomes dry and hard.
Beans and peanuts, wheat, rice, and corn are mature
seeds.

Mature seeds are not dead. We call them *dormant,*
or sleeping.

A seed is a storehouse of life. Each one contains
an *embryo,* a tiny living spot, from which the new
plant begins. The embryo has special parts that will
grow roots and others that will grow shoots to make
stems and leaves.

The embryo is only a tiny part of each seed. Around the embryo and attached to it is a food supply, called the *endosperm.* In it are *carbohydrates, proteins,* and *fats,* the necessary foods for a new growing plant.

Over the outside of each seed a hard coat protects the embryo and the endosperm. Without this outer cover many seeds would be ruined by the drying sun and the wind.

Seeds provide food for people and animals. Some seeds, such as nuts, may be eaten just as they are with only the hard shells, or seed coats, removed. We cook bean and pea seeds to make them soft enough to eat. Millers grind wheat seeds into flour. From this flour, bakers make bread, crackers, cakes, and cookies.

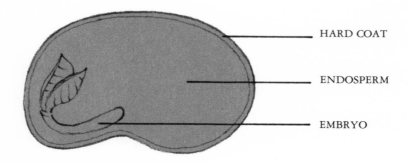

HARD COAT

ENDOSPERM

EMBRYO

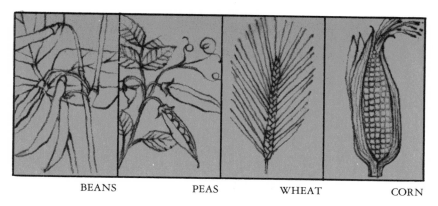

BEANS   PEAS   WHEAT   CORN

Breakfast cereals come from seeds of wheat, corn, oats, barley, and rye. We cook rice seeds to make them soft enough to eat. The fluffy white popcorn we enjoy as a special treat is the exploded seeds of a certain kind of corn.

Oil for cooking and to make margarine is pressed from corn, safflower, cotton, peanut, soybean, and coconut seeds.

Corn, wheat, and other seeds make much of the

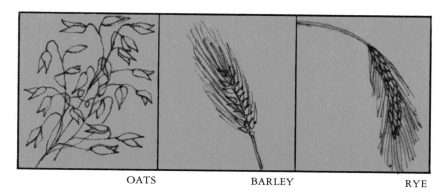

OATS   BARLEY   RYE

23

RICE　　　　　SAFFLOWER　　　　　COTTON

food for cows, pigs, and chickens. From these animals come meat, milk, and eggs.

Even though we eat many food seeds, people save enough to grow more plants. Flowers, weeds, trees, and shrubs usually have enough seeds to feed birds and other wild animals and to grow new plants.

How do seeds make new plants? How does a dry, dormant seed turn into a green plant, blossoming into a bright marigold or reaching toward the sky as a towering pine tree?

PEANUTS　　　　　SOY BEANS　　　　　COCONUT

24

WILD ROSE   HAWTHORNE

5 Plants from Seeds

Many seeds must have a dormant time when they will not *germinate,* or begin to grow. Where winters are cold, a seed that falls to the ground in autumn usually does not germinate until the next spring. Think what would happen if it did. The first fall frost would kill the tiny plant. It could not grow, bloom, and make more seeds. That kind of plant would quickly disappear from the earth.

Seeds of hawthorns, wild roses, and many other plants must have winter cold before they will germinate.

25

In spring the soil warms. Snow melts and rain falls. The seed coats *absorb,* or soak up, water. Inside each seed, the embryo swells and grows a hair-like root and a tiny shoot. Fed by the food stored in the endosperm, the shoot breaks through the seed coat and reaches upward toward the light. The root pushes down into the soil to get water with dissolved minerals.

Finally the plant comes through the soil surface. There it turns green. Sunlight and carbon dioxide in the air help the tiny plant to make food so it can grow larger.

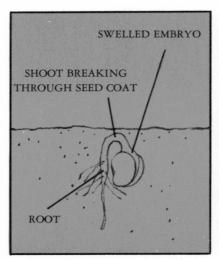
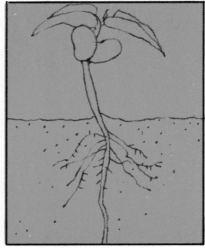

PUSSYWILLOW

In warm climates, seeds may germinate almost any time. The most likely time for new plants to appear is right after rain.

Some seeds stay alive a very short time. Others will live for many years. Pussywillow seeds live about ten days. If they fall from the tree onto dry soil, they die without germinating. But the seeds of a common weed, lamb's quarter, have stayed alive for as long as seventeen hundred years. The life of most seeds is somewhere between these two.

If seeds have especially hard coats, they must be deeply scratched to let water into their embryos, for every seed must have water to germinate. In woods and countryside, rocks, soil, trees, and other seeds rub and scratch seed coats. Animals walk on seeds,

LAMB'S QUARTER

cracking their coats and burying some of them in the soil. Many are ruined or lost, but more than enough escape to grow into new plants.

Here is a way to watch a seed become a plant.

See if you can get twelve bean seeds. Large lima beans are best. Cut six one-quart milk cartons to make pots three inches tall. Punch two holes into the bottom of each carton. Fill them with soil to within one-half inch of the top. Push two bean seeds down one inch into the soil of each carton. Water them thoroughly. Put the cartons into a shallow pan or tray on a warm, sunny windowsill. Number them from 1 to 6. Keep the soil damp, but not soaking wet.

After four days empty the soil from carton number 1. Look at the beans. What is happening to them?

In four more days carefully empty carton number 2 and look closely at the beans. See how they are changing.

Continue to empty one carton every four days, always taking the next number. What is happening?

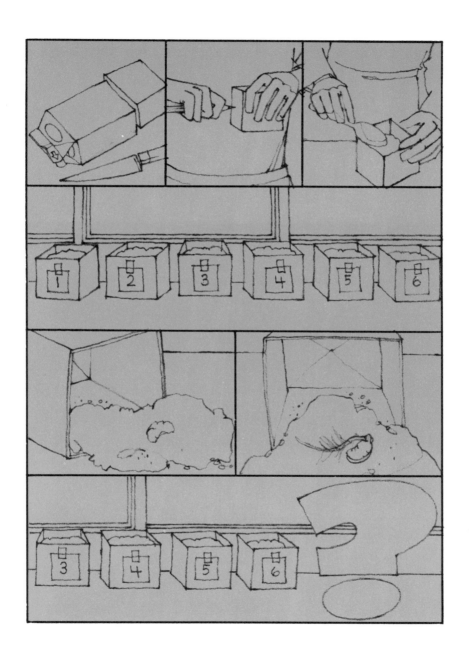

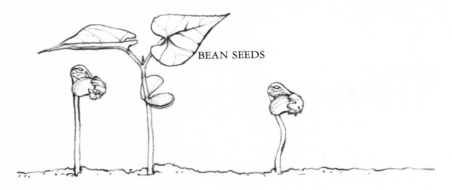

BEAN SEEDS

Notice how the two halves of the bean seed grow out of the soil and cling to the stems of the tiny plants. These halves are the endosperm of the bean seeds. They turn green in the sunlight to manufacture more plant food. Then they shrivel and fall off as new leaves grow to act as the plant's food factory.

Seeds grow in many sizes, shapes, and colors. Orchid seeds, the smallest of all, are like fine dust. Coconut seeds, the world's largest, sometimes weigh over thirty pounds each. Between these two we find seeds of many sizes and all of them have ways to move around the earth.

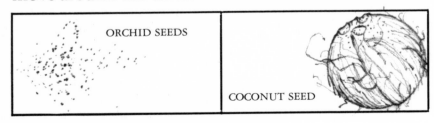

ORCHID SEEDS

COCONUT SEED

6 Flying Seeds

We know that pollen is often carried long distances. Seeds travel, too. How do they get from one place to another?

Perhaps you have picked white, fuzzy dandelion heads. When you hold a dandelion head in the wind, what happens? Pick one and blow on it. Watch the fuzz float away and fall to the ground in different places. Some may sail high into the sky.

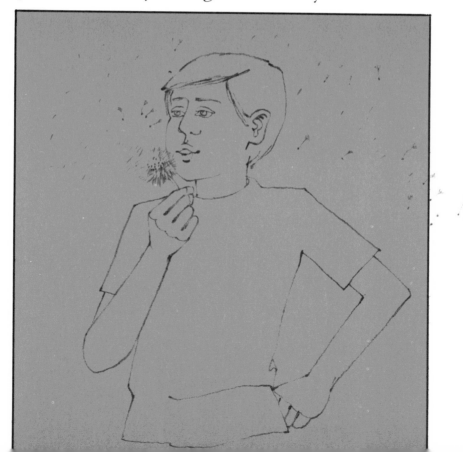

Hanging from the center of each bit of dandelion fuzz is a stalk with a very small seed at the end. When the seeds mature, these stalks break off the parent plant and the seeds sail into the air, flying on white parachutes. Seeds may fall to earth many miles from the places where they grew. There they germinate to grow into more dandelion plants.

Each dandelion head has many seeds. Maybe five out of every hundred find a place to grow. Some germinate but die before they bloom. Insects and birds eat some seeds and tiny plants. Still, enough remain to grow into new plants.

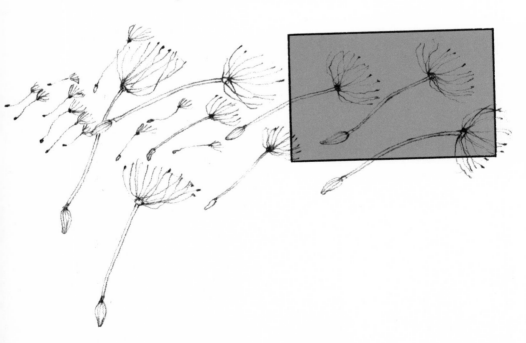

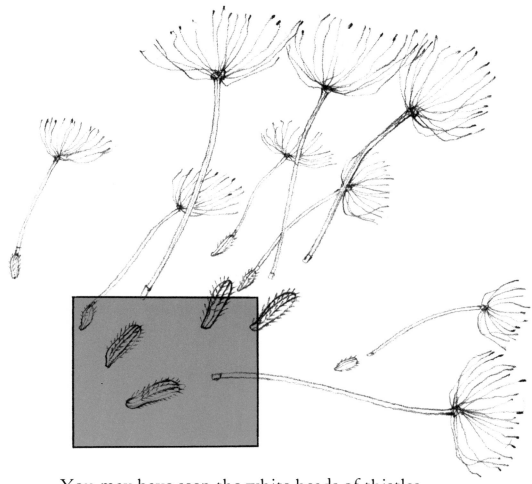

You may have seen the white heads of thistles
growing along roadsides in autumn. Like
dandelions, thistles fly on seed parachutes. Many
other common plants scatter their seeds by
parachute.

Have you seen maple seeds flying and dancing in a high wind? Pick one up from the ground or catch it as it flutters through the air. See the two seeds together, each with a wing like bird wings. On windy days they sail like toy gliders far from the maple tree. They stick in grass and fallen leaves until warm spring showers start new plants growing from them.

ENLARGED MAPLE SEED

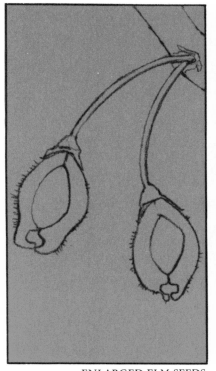

ENLARGED ELM SEEDS

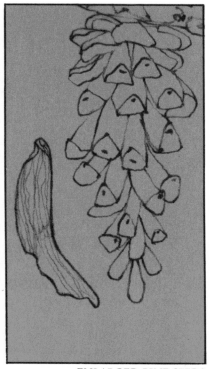

ENLARGED PINE SEEDS

Elm seeds grow in clusters, each with a thin fin or rudder. They spin as they fly away with the wind.

Small pine seeds drift from opened cones in autumn. Each has a paper-thin wing that whirls through the air as the seeds float to earth. They may rest on the forest floor or fall into cracks in the soil. Some of the seeds germinate to grow into tall trees.

35

BIRCH TREE

Perhaps you live near a birch tree that sends its millions of tiny, winged seeds flying like snow on the autumn wind.

Very fine seeds are blown about by the wind. Seeds of the dainty white flower, baby's breath, blow like sand. Tall foxgloves grow from dust-like seeds. Some very light grass seeds blow about, too. Bluebells and big rhododendron bushes grow from seeds as fine as sand, seeds that the wind carries over the countryside.

BABY'S BREATH FOXGLOVE BLUEBELL RHODODENDRON

ENLARGED HEATHER SEED

ENLARGED CLOVER SEED

Other wind-scattered seeds ride in little sacks full of air, sailing high into the sky like toy balloons. Heather seeds and some clover seeds grow balloons to help them fly.

Have you ever seen tumbleweeds piled against a fence or rolling across the road on a windy day? Tumbleweeds grow like round balls, tangled masses of stems and seeds. When they mature, the main stem breaks from the root. Wind rolls the

TUMBLEWEED

37

tumbleweeds across the country. With every turn, seeds break off and scatter. Some tumbleweed seeds have thorns that cling to everything the traveling plant touches.

Tumbleweeds nearly always grow in dry, open country. You see them in the western United States. One tumbleweed can scatter more than a thousand seeds.

If you live where tumbleweeds grow, get one of the plants just when it is ready to break off and roll away. Hang the tumbleweed from a cord or string in a dry place. After a few days, tap it gently. What happens? Shake it, as a high wind would shake it. Watch the seeds fall.

Seeds are prize aviators. They fly on the wind as dust, with wings, parachutes, fins, and balloons, or they roll over the earth. As they go they help spread seeds around the world.

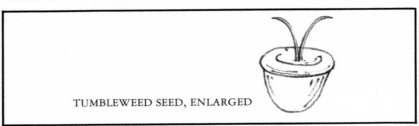

TUMBLEWEED SEED, ENLARGED

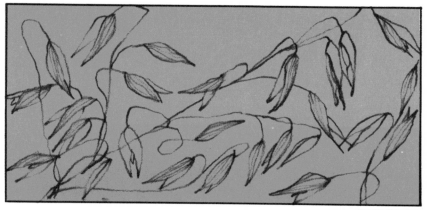

OAT SEEDS

7 Self-Moving Seeds

People and animals move about on their legs. Some seeds can move themselves, too. Tiny hairs, bristles, or claws grow on their outside edges or at one end of each seed. When dew and rain wet these seeds they swell and the spines or claws grip the soil. The seeds move slightly. Then they dry again until the next damp night or shower helps them crawl a bit farther. At last, the seeds stick into the soil and grow. Seeds of many desert plants, oat seeds, and some clover seeds creep over the soil.

Clematis seeds both creep and fly. This flowering vine has seeds that blow about on twisted spines. When rain falls, the spines swell and the seeds fall to earth to crawl along the ground.

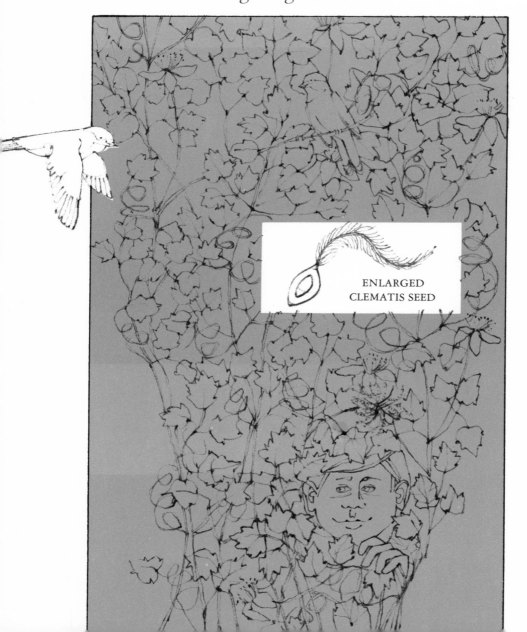

ENLARGED
CLEMATIS SEED

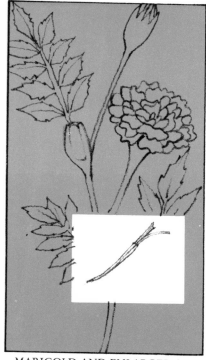

MUSTARD AND ENLARGED SEED   MARIGOLD AND ENLARGED SEED

Mustard and marigold seeds get sticky when they are wet. They glue themselves to the ground so they cannot move. Marigold seeds have more glue on the rooting end. They blow over the soil and come to rest with this end sticking firmly to the soil. Water causes the seeds to swell and work their way down. The seeds germinate, firmly anchored in the ground.

41

MANGROVE BUSH

Scrubby mangrove bushes grow in salty, tropical marshlands. Their seeds germinate while they are still on the plants. As each seed swells it becomes heavy, breaks off, and plops deep into the mud below, where it grows into a new mangrove plant.

Impatiens, or touch-me-not, grows along streams and in gardens in most of North America. If you touch a ripe seed pod, it will burst open and shoot the seeds away.

IMPATIENS WITH POD

SNAPPER AND MATURE SEEDS, ENLARGED

A plant called snappers grows on pine trees in the western United States. If you strike a branch when the seeds are mature, they explode like toy guns, scattering in all directions.

Each purple needlegrass seed has a long twisted barb at one end. Water unwinds this barb, pushing the seed into the soil. Many grasses of the plains and prairies plant their own seeds.

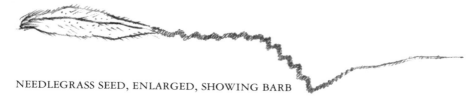

NEEDLEGRASS SEED, ENLARGED, SHOWING BARB

A few plants have seeds that grow in the soil. Most common of these strange plants is the peanut. In many countries, peanuts are called groundnuts because they grow underground. Flowers bloom at the tops of the peanut plants. After a flower is fertilized, the ovary sends out a narrow tube that grows down into the soil. Seeds mature under the plant. Any seeds the farmer or digging ground squirrels miss may grow into more peanut plants.

Seeds move about in many ways. They fall to the

PEANUTS

44

soil where they become mixed into it. How many seeds can we find in soil? Scrape two tablespoons of earth from the top on a roadside or in a vacant lot. Spread a double layer of paper toweling over a plastic one-pound coffee can lid or another lid or saucer of about the same size. Spread your collected soil evenly over the towel-covered lid. Wet it thoroughly. Place the lid on a warm windowsill. Look at it every day. Be sure to keep it damp. After a few days, you should see tiny green plants pushing their tips upward. Keep the soil until no more plants appear. Count the plants. The seed for every plant that grew was in the soil you collected.

8 Floating Seeds

Think what a hard rainstorm might do to mature seeds. A wheat field, ripe for harvest, can be flattened by driving rain. Heavy seed heads break off. Water washes them about.

In autumn, after many seeds mature, go outside after a rainstorm. If you live in a city, dip a can or cup of muddy water from the gutter. Try to get it

near a park or where plants grow along the street. In the country collect the water along a road. Take it home and strain it through a piece of thin cloth. What is left? There are pebbles, mud, some leaves, but what else?

Let us find out if there were any seeds in the muddy water. Spread the soil, pebbles, and whatever else is left in the cloth over a lid or saucer that you have first covered with a paper towel. Put it in a

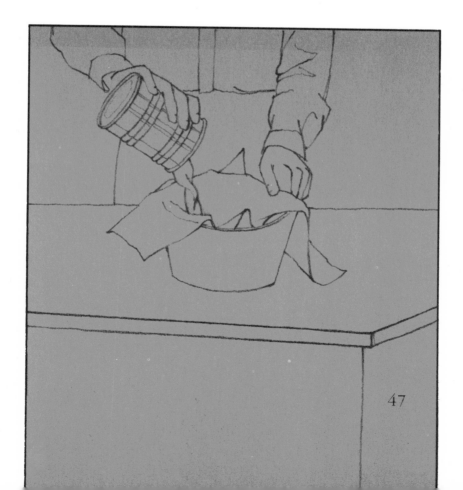

warm place and keep it damp. In a few days you may
see plants growing from seeds that traveled in the
gutters with the rain water.

If you had not collected these seeds, they might
have floated into creeks and rivers and even into the
ocean.

48

Plants that grow on beaches shed their seeds onto the sand, where tides wash them out to sea. Their pods, often full of air like balloons, float on the water. They come to rest on distant beaches where they germinate and grow. Beach plants are the prize travelers of the plant world.

Water, whether it comes as rain, in streams, or in oceans, helps spread seeds and plants around the earth.

9 Hitchhiking Seeds

People, birds, and other animals carry seeds from place to place. Some seeds have burrs and barbs that cling to fur, wool, and clothing.

Have you seen cocklebur seeds stuck to a dog's coat? When the dog scratches, the seeds may fall to the ground to grow, probably far away from the place where the dog found them. The seeds hitch-hiked in his fur. Your dog may also get sharp-pointed foxtail seeds in his fur and ears. Many grass seeds travel about stuck to animals and to clothing.

COCKLEBUR

FOXTAIL

Filaree, a common plant in pastures and ranges in the western United States and in other parts of the world, has seeds with barbs that point backward like the barbs on a fish hook. They cling to animal fur and sometimes work their way to the skin. They also ride about in the wool of sheep and in our clothing.

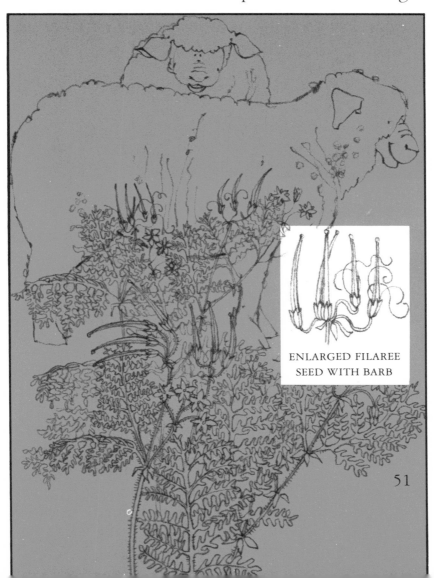

ENLARGED FILAREE
SEED WITH BARB

51

ENLARGED
STICK-TIGHT SEED

ENLARGED
BURR CLOVER SEED

If you walk in the woods or through a country meadow in autumn, you are likely to find small barbed seeds sticking to your socks and trousers. Some, perhaps, are stick-tights or devil's darning-needles.

Maybe some burr-clover seeds stuck to your socks. Round and flat, each seed has a circle of prickly spines around the outside.

If you walked in a sandy place, you may have collected sharp-barbed sandburs in your clothing. All these seeds hitch rides from place to place.

Have you seen ants carry seeds, marching in a line like soldiers? Colonies of ants found in Texas collect and plant grass seeds. When their fields mature, they carry the seeds to their nests. Some of the seeds grow into new grass plants.

Birds carry seeds about, losing some that they intended to eat. Ducks, gulls, and other shore birds collect seeds in mud that sticks to their feet. Then they fly to other places where the seeds wash or fall off.

ENLARGED SANDBUR

Gluey seeds stick to fur and feathers. As animals move about, or birds fly and swim, the seeds fall to the ground.

Animals and birds eat fruits, especially berries, which hold ripe seeds. The seeds fall to the soil in droppings and may germinate far from the places where they grew.

People move seeds, too. We trade seeds with other countries. They may travel in ships, on trains, in trucks, or in airplanes.

Weed seeds travel around the world in shoes and other clothing. Hay for animals and straw for packing hold seeds that cross land and sea.

Try to get a seed catalog. See how many different seeds the company sells. If you order seeds, they will be mailed to you and delivered by the postman, just one more way that seeds travel.

In 1883, the small island of Krakatau in the East Indies exploded, shooting lava and smoke into the air. After many days, the volcano cooled, leaving a bare island. Nothing grew there.

Three years later, scientists counted twenty-four wind-blown plants growing on Krakatau. More plants arrived as people, wind, the sea, birds, and other animals brought seeds from nearby islands. Fifty years after the volcano left the island bare, it was green with plants. Many things helped bring seeds to cover a bare patch of earth.

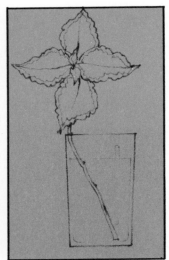

10 Plants from Plants

Not all plants grow from seeds. We can often start a
new plant from a piece of stem or stem and leaves.
These cuttings, or slips, will grow roots, then send
out new leaves.

If you would like to start a plant from a cutting,
get a small branch from a coleus plant. Coleus are
fancy-leaved green and red house plants. Take off all
but the top four leaves and put the stem into a small
glass of water. Put it in a light place out of the sun.
Add water as needed to keep the stem well covered.

After a few days look at the coleus stem. You should see tiny white roots. In about two weeks, the plant will have many roots. Pot the cutting in good garden soil or potting mixture from the supermarket. Use a flower pot or a cut-down half-gallon milk carton with two holes punched into the bottom of it. Place a saucer under your pot so water will not get on the table or windowsill and set it in a sunny place. Keep it damp. Before many weeks it will grow into a handsome plant with many colorful leaves.

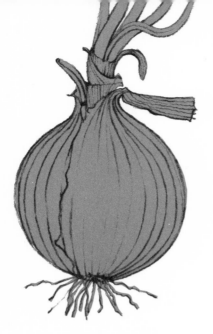

Some plants have thick stems, called bulbs. Bulbs store food and water for new plants. Onions are bulbs. Each layer of an onion is a dormant leaf. If you plant an onion, it will grow roots and green leaves.

Daffodils, tulips, and other lilies grow best from bulbs.

TULIPS   DAFFODILS

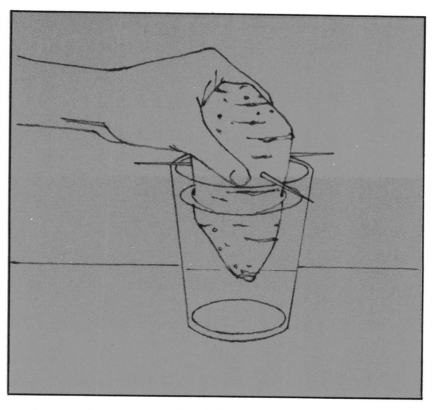

Some plants store food for new plants in thick underground stems called *tubers*. Both white and sweet potatoes are tubers. They will grow in water. If you would like to try it, get a sweet potato. Put the small end into a jar or glass. Cover about one-half of the tuber with water. Put it in a shady place for a week. Then bring it out into the sunshine.

Small green sprouts should be coming from the top. Add more water to keep the sweet potato half covered. Notice the roots in the water. In a few weeks you will have a bright green vine. Because the tuber holds a rich store of plant food, the vine will grow for a long time without soil.

Gardeners and nurserymen start most shrubs and trees from cuttings. A cutting always grows into a plant like its parent. Seeds of one kind of plant may produce very different seedlings, or new plants. This is because the ovary that grew into the seed was fertilized by pollen from a different plant. A seedling from a sweet, juicy peach may grow into a tree with sour, dry fruit.

Across the western United States and in the Rocky Mountain area, tall slender poplar trees line roads and ditches. Rows of poplars tell all who pass by that pioneers settled there. The pioneers cut small branches from poplar trees. They wrapped the

cuttings in wet cloth or put them into buckets of water and carried them in their wagons as they moved west. When the people found places to make their homes, the cuttings had roots. And the pioneers planted them. After a few years, the cuttings grew into tall trees, green in summer, golden in autumn.

All over the world plants grow. Flowers bloom, seeds form and mature. They travel about, germinate, and grow into new plants. Cuttings sprout leaves and roots and grow. As old plants die, new ones take their places. The many ways plants spread a green cover over the earth is one of nature's miracles—wonderful, indeed.

Index